Gather Light:

A Collection of Poems with an Autobiographical Work in Progress

James A Carter

Contents

Part I: A Collection of Poems

Gather Light

On certain days in October, we would gather light like fallen fruit,
But our baskets could not hold it. Only the odor of leaves,
Pungent and penetrating, stayed in the loose weave,
As we crunched our wayward path, strewing detritus
In our wake like windblown pixie dust.
But the red and the rust remained, staining baskets,
Staining fingers with the hope that always lingers
When autumn eats the sky, when geese begin their cry
Of leaving, when we are lost in paths of evening
Holding forlorn baskets dripping discarded light.

And So We Pray

And so we pray.
We pray that today is a testament to faith,
That knees will not lock nor sinews snap.
We pray for steps, small but certain,
Forward through a forest of doubt.
We pray for the bread and the blood as we fast;
For the broken branch and the bird in its nest.
We pray for the grain, for the mother's breast,
For the womb of incessant rain.
And so we pray;
We pray for the bosom of light,
For the nectar that sweetens the night.
We pray for the things unseen,
For the stain that scours us clean.

I Shall Believe

I shall believe the things I believe, for
believing makes them real:
The wheel cannot turn in its tourniquet of
rust,
The river cannot bend in its sleeve of silt,
The raven cannot build her nest of straw,
And the heart cannot break its burden of
blood.
I can believe the things I believe, for I have
seen them:
The face that forms in the tide of smoke,
The stem that stirs in the unplanted seed,
The sun that stuns the bee in flight,
The apple that burns in the angel's breast.
These are the embers igniting the crest,
The singing moon and the spooning wave,
The crisp calculation of the star-bleached
cave.
I choose to believe what my mind can see
When given the key to its dark reverie.

Praise Them

Praise the woods and the wetlands,
The umbilical tide in its turning,
Its unceasing ease in its nature, not human,
Uncaring, simple in itself.
Praise the forest and the unplowed field,
The stand of pine, erect with purpose,
Unpretentious, unthinking, essential
In its pursuit of lofty heights.
Praise the horse and the hapless human,
Seekers of God in brazen grandeur,
Golden in sun, sleek as marble,
One with the woods and the fields:
Praise them, even as sleek shadows
Devour them in darkling daylight.
Praise them.

Dog and Rook

Where do we sleep now when snow binds
the stable door,
When frost finds its way to the rafters and
the rookery
Mocks the morning?
Love does not find purchase in winter's
weak bones,
When the cracking and cawing ring the bell
and run.
The hayrick has gone sallow, the larder left
abandoned,
And the dog disappears in the virgin field
Chasing a solitary rook, frost-bound broken
wings
Sowing their fallow feathers as the
meadowlark sings.

Dead Tree

The dead tree at the edge of the wood is an
old man,
Arms ascending to heaven in final
supplication.
He trembles in winter wind, unfirm legs
Leaning this way, then that.
His once fat trunk tested by time, tenacious
still though tenuous.
I watch as brittle branches fall:
Fingers from a leper, mendicant with empty
bowl.
How do I now give him succor, shelter from
the fang-toothed storm,
Turn back time and tempest so his bark is
tender skin?
I watch and wait, his reflection growing dim
In the graying twilight pond.
When he cracks and falls, will I be here to
hear?

Eels Came Early

Eels came early this year; glass slivers from
Sargasso salt
Swimming through brine, finding freshwater
brook or pond
For miraculous purpose of growth.
This is not theory. This is faith:
Faith in birthright; faith in beginnings;
Faith in patience; faith in silence;
Faith in miracle.
For no matter how vast the sea,
And although they have no wings,
Nor speak with tongues of men,
In their own world they are angels.
Even if the ancients were right, if they rise
from mud and slime,
We too are but ash and dust, both rot and
rust,
Turning our own shade of yellow
Far from our own Sargasso.

Let Me Live in This Moment

Let me live in this moment when my eyes
are sealed in sleep,
When I cannot witness a tender face fade
into colorless linen.
Let the sweet but luring shadows breathe
with solemn lungs,
Unchaste and unholy in abandoned corners
and closets.
Let the unseen hand smooth the reticent
forelock
Hanging in mock surrender. Let the cool lips
linger
Long enough only to steal the escaping
breath
Stirring the purple heath.

Seasonal Urges

Too long for blood to be there still:
Stains that seep and cannot be scoured.
Flesh is all too pale to challenge seasonal
urges
Rising like rivers of redundancy,
Streams and brackish inlets running,
Slowly, so slowly,
Even in summer-heat.
But blood races, pulse steady,
Staining rich brocade,
Crimson Rorschach of unexpressed desire,
Firewater enkindling not dousing.
Water is not wine,
Wine is not blood,
And communion commences with an urge,
Stained yet unfulfilled.

Rest By the River

Come rest by the river before it recedes,
Before the rushes and reeds
Write their strict calligraphy against the
dying tide.
Paddle this patchwork canoe past rocks
And stumps of yawning reminiscence,
Out where the current is still,
Where the groaning of oarlocks grows calm.
Take measure with your human hand,
Bid the bastard land adieu.
Walk to the water's edge--
Blessed, broken, and born anew.

I Am Made of Breath

I am made of breath, exhalation of atoms.
Perhaps some Sunday morning when the
sermon is done,
I shall be mist, mercurial and lithe, rising
with the grace of things
Unseen, all vapor and cloud, comely in the
way lovers once were.
And the ghost shall grace the bread; living
and the dead
Gathered in air thin as mercury stillness,
silent as spores
In unmown field, ancient as atoms of
Original Sin.
And evening shall find me, slow dark
descending
Over fields of moving mist, ghosts calling
from shadows,
Voices of vapor and cloud calling the lost
lover
To break bread in the silent breathing grace.

Mute Impressions

While giving the wall a fresh coat of paint, I snapped the fourth rung
And fell to the parquet floor. The seal on the paint split open,
Crimson contents spreading like plague-bearing armies
Riding pale horses, or butterflies on broken glass,
Or azaleas bleeding in the open palm of Spring.
Unfazed and uneven, it edged closer and closer
To fringes of the jewel-tone carpet.
And I--prone, impotent witness--submerged a mute finger,
Red now with the ancient curse of blood,
No brother here to bear the cruel stigmata.

No Roses Here

Do not stray into my garden; there are no
roses here,
And the open gate is not an invitation to
pilfering.
Choose instead my neighbor, whose nether
paths
Are paved with finest sandstone, and whose
pear trees
Hang with scented blossoms and red, ripe
fruit.
My patchwork parcel is strewn with rotting
plums
And apricots unappealing to taste or smell.
I have cultivated here with deliberate care,
Feeding the weeds and withered stalks
Like urchins in a cautionary tale.
A poor thing, but mine own...my garden
Still glistens when the moon is full
And lost bouquet of roses rides on the tide's
last pull.

Luna Moth

I covet the green of the Luna moth,
The rich textured cloth hiding its throat,
The unbuttoned coat of its wings.
Even when the nightingale sings, its songs
Do not entrance, neither the leaping dance
Of swans from the ruffled lake.
But the cool green of wings such peace
brings,
I covet nothing more. Legend and lore
Speak of change, the grace of embracing the
strange,
Accepting the things carried by wings
Of angel, bird, or moth: small wonders spun
from cloth
That warm the soul and maketh the
splintered whole.

All Things Bleed

All things bleed when pricked: sapling or
savior,
The ooze is not contained.
Suffering, for some, comes easy,
Natural as the embryonic flight of starlings
On a brisk afternoon in October,
Weather and witchery notwithstanding.
Sacrifice, for some, is safe--
Gnarled knot in the pine plank
Breaking the teeth of the saw.
Play this out in your mind, I say:
Pin-prick of the needle on flesh,
Willing or unwelcome, all is the same.
Blood is blood, shed in silence or scream,
On cross of callous wood, or silk sheets in
autumn dream.

Dream of Balance

We dream of balance, ball on index finger spinning,
Spare moments--sparse and tender--rendered in words
Spun like silk, silk brocade of an axis failing, falling,
Falling into desultory dream,
For only in dream is there balance:
Time unbroken, time moving in symmetry,
Symmetry of lost worlds, worlds out of time,
Out of transition, out of the persistence of time itself.
In dream, the ball spins faster and faster,
World unlashed from mainmast, ship aground,
Sentinels failing, free-fall of all that is holy.
Yet still we dream, day or night, in sleep or awake,
Awaiting balance, ball now rolling with volition,
With trajectory, rolling toward the reckoning,
When the dreamer awakens and the brocade
Lies folded at the foot of the unmade bed.

This Weathered Coat

What shall become of this weathered coat--
Rustic threadbare rag--when witches brew
And hemlock stew steep into blood and
bone?
O the marrow shall reek and cells shall
speak,
Screaming empirical lies. Dog days shall
pass
With an aching frown; hayfields unmown
Shall tempt the blade dull as aging dreams.
What tales shall lie unwaxed, waning now
In the fat sun that comes only once?
What bargain shall I reject, what hindsight
Box of miracles of elements bare and base?
But I know in my heart the kindest course:
I shall trade this weathered winter coat
For the blanket that warms the horse.

White Wolf

When the white wolf paused at the perimeter
Of the garden, I watched like a voyeur
His primeval nocturnal necromancy;
Throwing his head back, he howled
To the mute immutable heavens
The surplus of pain in his
Primordial canine heart.
Man or wolf: all is the same--
Blood burning under the ripeness
Of a moon that pulls the inland
Tide of blood to its very margins.
I take to all-fours, sniffing the
Gray ground alive with sensate smell--
The hint of the hare just-gone.
Autumnal mist hangs thick as gnats
In the gnawing October air.
I too shall yield no quarter;
Not one--no, not any--shall find
Hearth or haven--shelter from
Lycanthropic license, inchoate
Harbinger of mayhem and unrest,
Ancient and unyielding call of blood.
This ghostly Rorschach revealing
Twisted gametes of a hybrid heart:
Shapeshifter at Winifred's Well
Scrubbing the moon from his skin.

You, Stranger

You, stranger, confined to your Little Ease,
What pleases your eyes now that the veil is
torn?
What years have you suspended in
sacrificial jelly,
What has filled your belly but lust,
And the rust that arrives with doubt?
If now, you were let out, set free from the
carnal,
What obligatory silence would enshroud
you?
Your tongue trapped in teeth of stone,
No words to atone for your usury,
No prayer to offer, no dirt to daub the scabs
Of remorse caked on your cloying soul.
The blood-doomed bowl shelters a pale
repast
Before bedtime and an aging, insufferable
fast.

Self-Portraits

Sit, love, let us paint ourselves,
Self-portraits of unpromise leaking pastel shades
On faces melting as morning ages.
Before the light fades, before the primrose withers,
Let us choose our careful palette, colors honest
As words our hearts have hidden.
Canvas stretched and taut awaiting the brush
Banishing lines and creases crafted by another hand.
But our well-placed swirls and delicate daubs
Are no defense against the wound and willing
Swiss movements measured and precise
Plucking the fine bristles from brushes
Locked in fingers bearing pastel stains
Weak spirits cannot erase.

My Steps Are Slow

My steps are slow but deliberate,
Especially in the silent swamp
That yields no echo of their falling.
Feet know the accustomed path,
The pattern of leaves, the patina of bark
Rough and ancient as unshared myths.
Especially in morning, when mist
Lies like a coat of contextual color,
Unbroken, unspeaking, yet crisp
As the crackle of crows.
Steps are deliberate and slow,
One, then another, placed with precision
Of memory, fixed in untangled amber;
Three, then more, moorings now tested
With tightly wound strands of shadow,
Shade, and silence, keeping the whole from
dissolving.
Steps are slow and deliberate
On this path of frail remembrance.

After Sleep

After sleep comes the waking;
No, not awakening, for that is a different
thing.
The clover that covers the field grows in
steady increase;
Patterns form and fade as eyes open to
undreamed day.
Sleep is the longing, the yearning crimped
by age,
By antique ritual of chalice and chanting.
Sleep is the broken finger, always bent,
Always pointing to an uncaptured end
Floating now in dandelion stillness.
And yet the clover grows, silent and steady,
Awaiting the waking hand, the waking heart
Released at last from sleep's unyielding
sanctum.

Dover Beach Revisited

Dover Beach was calm
When Arnold felt the spray on his palm
And mourned the ebbing of Faith.
But I stand on the shore of another
continent,
In a different century,
And celebrate the sea's indifference.
Yes, love, we are true to one another,
But truth has no steadfast boundaries.
Here beneath the crescent moon
That shone on Sophocles and Attila alike,
A different alignment speaks.
For a moment, we are molecules,
Empty mollusks cast on the barren sand
Beneath the glow of star and horned moon.
Waves betoken the movement of centuries;
Try as we may, we cannot beat back
That unconquerable army of salt and foam,
That juggernaut of eternal engine,
Repository of rage and regret.
But I am not Caligula; my arrogance
Stems from a different source.
Beneath the night sky with its
Occasional postings of light,
The blank sea is no mocking mirror:
My face disappears in its fathoms,
Frozen in death's lethargy.
Let this be the lesson of such
Tender and tenacious nights:

Time engulfs time; Age digests age.
Only the armless starfish remains.

They Cut the Chain

They cut the chain that turned the wheel;
No longer would it move in slow, smooth
mockery
Of the slow, smooth moving earth.
Pedals once in willful rotation, now frozen,
Stationary as stalactites in a cave of
nocturnal memory.
Here there is no rhythm, no rejoicing in
perfect, round,
Orbital observance. And so the world ends:
Nothing rendered but stillness--
Silence of the once turning wheel.

Utopia Redux

Do not press these paling petals in the pages
of Thomas More.
Roses and baby's breath will only stain his
saintly prose
And befoul an already jaded nose with
palliating spores,
Crimson secretions and covert seepings
more fit for tomb
Or sepulcher than residing here in a scholar's
room.
Take these withered stems of woe
And bury them where they will not grow
Into bines and tethered branches choking
breath
From leathered tomes; detach this deathly
myopia
Lest it despoil tender leaves of a budding
utopia.

When I Was Naked and Newborn

When I was naked and newborn, I nailed my palms to a tree
As my supper grew cold in the acrid afterbirth.
When I was a spindle of silence, the whip cracked loud and long
As my feet curled in coils of snakes deep in the barking dawn.
And the womb was a breaking fever, chilblains of rising waste.
When I was free and feral, God was a mewling pup
Stretching his chain in the doorless dog pound yard.
When I was a beakless bird, the worm was a weathervane
Turning and twisting in caverns of cirrus clouds.
And winter became spring in petals of pealing rain.

Too Wet for Fire

Wood was too wet for fire; kindling would not catch
In the dripping hours of daylight. We gathered what colors
We could find--ocher and umber--to unlock the knuckles
Frozen in pale and unthawing pigments, unforgiving
In their hold. But warm and willing hues
Could not unfreeze fingers stiff as masonry,
Cold now to the touch, longing for blood-love,
For beginner's luck in the loose and listening
Hound-loud shank of dripping daylight.
But flesh was too tame for fire, kindling could not spark
Loose colors expending spores in cellars dank and dark.

The Hunger

How shall I sate this thirst for your body and
your blood?
And though the heart is tough to teeth and
tongue,
It is a tender instrument. I cannot stop its
pulsing,
Its beating, free falling in bone-bent cage.
But love's labor demands consumption:
Unhurried hunger for the last meal,
The final repast before time withers urge,
Before salt and brine pollute desire,
And vinegar smothers sweetbreads.
How shall I consume the dead bitter vetch
Pretending it is honey to the taste?
I shall leave this heart in its place of waste,
Soothe the tongue with love's low speech.

That Night I Found You

That night I found you freezing, blue
With God in the greenhouse,
I rinsed my face in the pail of moonlight,
And the silver beams stayed on my skin.
Though enchanted by your dalliance,
Forgiveness could not be granted,
Not even if you were fondled by godhead,
Deity's seed still fresh on your thighs.
I could not compete with blistering eyes
Eating a hole in your heart,
Nor with your seething womb
Transformed into unholy art.

Angels' Share

These fingers--leaf-form and frail--have
burst their bark,
Dividing the rough-cut nails like
unburnished diamonds.
Dreams confined to lifeline dance across
skin
Once taut and thick as a thicket.
Tumbler leaves a strict tattoo in the palm--
Embedded, etched...a mirrored gemstone
pattern.
Ice melts, diluting the scent of bourbon,
Water and whiskey mixing in weak
remembrance
Of properties of taste and texture.
Old limb trembles as shards tinkle,
Disguising a once rich bouquet.
This is the tragic stillness at end of day,
Beyond reason, beyond confines of care.
All that remains is angels' share.

Days of Dying Leaves

These days of dying leaves, I do not stray
from home.
The womb and the wasp have their
comforts,
Though the sting of both is deep.
In sleep I count the colors, falling ecstasy of
light, broken remnants,
Reminiscent of passion and pubescent lore.
What lies in store from here, when daylight
comes,
My heart can only guess. Shall I dress
To mock the maple, the morning pitch
Of senses attuned to flock and fleece?
Shall I turn my ears to the honking of geese
Trailing their skyward path?
Or shall I stay indoors, safe from the
seasons,
Safe from the leaves, safe from the wrath
That arrives with unstated reasons?
No, I shall not stray from home
In this dawn of dying leaves.

For the Seizing

I have honed these knives for the flensing,
handles of intricate bone,
Flesh now ripe for the seizing.
Across the fields mist is lifting, hills like
humpbacks
Riding wheat-waves in ethereal sun of
morning.
Here and there, but mostly there, sweet blue
buds
Spring from thawing earth, open in their
time,
Recede again in another age.
As shadows melt from the rough-hewn
porch,
I ask no more of morning than a handle of
scrimshaw
Pressed against my palm and ancestral flesh
Ripened now for the seizing.

Nocturnal Embers

Days of blazing heaven, burned and
bristling
In the heat-spun shaft of evening,
When nocturnal embers of remembrance
Stain the stories we tell, tales we embellish
In the retelling. And if we choose to dance
In this dim light of melancholy expectation,
How shall we find our feet, our loose
habitation
Harbored in ashes only? In the reliving,
The retelling, we will be a whirl of bodies,
Spectral forms on floors untouched,
Ashes of angels in half-light shaft of
evening.

Smoke and Antique Paper

Love, you said, smells of smoke and antique paper,
But love is now the paper reduced to smoldering ash
In the heat of your resentment. All is travesty--
Transient rain drops staining a delicate rose
Like silk brocade from another century.
The purple sky lights up and breaks,
As if pain were not sufficient, not enough
To tear the intricate lining of days too deeply buried.
Even shadows grow pale in the banshee
Presence of this gray ghost that haunts the heart's cold corridors,
Leaving the doors ajar, exposing abandoned salons that resounded once
With the banter and passion of youth.
Play for me a song on strings stretched taut and tender--
Plaintive lament to resurrect the long-dead human animal,
Or perhaps a dirge will do, and the dead shall bury the dead.
November was my nonage, August an epiphany.

And all the days between--casualties of a bloodless battle.
Some things are true of love and war:
Truth is the first casualty in both;
Veracity a corpse picked by the vulture's beak,
Until all that is left is the lie.
Words blow away like cannon smoke,
Disperse in the wind like strangers
Departing a commuter train,
Running for a cab to shield them
From the persistent pelting rain.

Totems

We are as we say we are: totems of uneasy resistance
To forces divine and demonic. Leaves fall like hail
From a heaven of barren boughs, arms reaching
For the child fatherless on an altar of unyielding stone.
But bone can be split only by axe, not axiom.
"*Respice Finem*," coos the flesh,
Hymn of neither comfort nor joy.
Where now does the mother seek the lost boy,
In forest or in fen, beneath barren boughs
Casting no shadow in day's slow descent?
Wolf tooth punctures the lung,
Ants coat the once febrile tongue:
Totems of uneasy reluctance
On an altar of unyielding chance.

I Cut Out My Heart…

I cut out my heart this morning,
Placed it raw and still beating
On the kitchen cutting board.
Taking the sharpest paring knife,
I peeled back its layers
Hoping to find within…what?
A word? An image? A memory perhaps
To justify its idiotic habit
Of sustaining life in a dung-heap?
With perversion of purpose,
I gripped the bone handle
Of the perfectly balanced knife,
And pinned that throbbing organ
Like a lepidopterist's specimen
To the stained and unyielding wood.
But still it would not stop,
Its rhythmic beating a bloodless mockery,
A cruel echoing conceit:
I must live without my heart
Yet guided by its beat.

Things We Tell Ourselves

Things we tell ourselves in the dark cannot
be voiced in the light.
When the incoherent god of the gut--treason
of the senses--
Stirs crosscurrents, vagaries of commitment,
pulling, not pushing,
Seasonal changes at the core.
Shoreline recedes, but the past does not
change.
And this petty arrangement of cells divides,
divides again:
Newness is not always welcome.

Tight Shoes

"Tight shoes," he said, before pausing for effect,
"Were given us by God to test our mettle,
To test our power of choice, a testament to free will.
If we choose to walk in them, toes cribbed and confined,
We take circumstance upon ourselves,
Eschewing comfort for mendacity. But..."
Here he relit the meerschaum pipe, pulled a deep puff,
Furrowed his brow and continued.
"But if we choose to loosen the laces that bind
The manmade manacles chafing our ankles, then...
Then *we* become as God, freeing our blistered feet
From leatherbound bonds. Better the stones and the briars
Punishing our unshackled soles..."
His voice trailed off, the lesson complete,
As he slipped into sleep, discarded slippers
Tossed like flotsam on the polished cedar floor.

Sea Change

Light was on the water as wave, then wave
swept
Fierce angles in the blue bones of my face.
Seized by whitecaps and roiling weather,
Muscle and ligament broke in unison,
As barnacles bled in half-light,
Eyes empty to the staring, edgeless sky.
Terns and petrels plowed their even furrows
In the frozen, unspeaking sea,
And I was Jonah spit from the bile-slick
slime
Of whale and water, lone mariner
Drifting on the deadwood wreck of time.

When She Slept

When she slept, if she slept at all, only
French linen would sheathe her.
Enveloped in softness above and beneath
her, only the owls
And the stillborn rain could close her eyes
and still the steady pulse
Of longing and regret. Even when her
feathers froze in the wet
Wild night of lingering stars and comets
crashing like waves,
She would wrap herself in sweet comfort:
white linen cocoon
Shining like silver beneath a breathing,
broken moon.

Blood Cleansing

Blood on my face in the mirror;
Blood on the bathroom floor;
Blood on the face of the moon.
Bird that chirps at the window
Gurgles through gouts of blood.
Corn that I shuck in the kitchen
Spurts like a severed vein.
Lemon in its wanton fullness
Leaves its menstrual ooze
On the tips of my crimson fingers.
Blood from the copper kettle
Stains the porcelain cup.
Only the wine is clear:
Claret with translucence of water.
How shall I become clean?

One Small Step

When Armstrong left the imprint of his sole
In the dust of the lunar surface and uttered
His well-rehearsed line that floats still above
That barren landscape like a child's balloon
Caught in the rib-cage rafters of a suburban
mall,
He sentenced the remainder of us to earth-
imposed exile,
Limited to our well-charted land like lions
Pacing the perimeters of a cage that grows
More confining with each uneasy pass,
Leaving its imprint on our soul.

No Best Days

There are no best days, only some days
better than others:
When the choking moon is manifest in the
pre-evening sky;
When the saffron butterfly swims with
elemental ease;
When the green of the grass is more
gorgeous than all human faces
Of frailty and forgetfulness, of mortality and
wan expectation;
When even the creaking of boards and bones
cannot o'er shade the simple.
No, there are no best days, but those rare
days better than others
Are charms, pure as periwinkle on lawns
long gone in the loosening.

When Angels Tire of Us

When angels tire of us,
They sleep in flowers disguising themselves as bees,
Saffron halos slipping to their midriff.
In the frail remains of broken petals, they breathe,
Stirring pollen with each exhalation.
And in their quiet slumber, they dream of the hive,
Alive with the buzz of holiness, honey in the comb.
When the afternoon wanes, light fading to shadow,
Bright wings sing and air is thick with unseen bodies
Flying in tight formation seeking again the lost and forlorn,
Spreading their holy dust in sweet dew of Eden's first morn.

Broken Boy

The egg cracked, and the broken boy ran,
Ran into the fire where the air was sweet
And smelled of jasmine and lavender.
He wrapped himself in sage and smoke,
Holier now than membrane, than memory
Persisting through pleasures rough and
beguiling.
Longing to embrace, he could not foresee
His arms were kindling, bare and burning
In the nucleus of his dreams: legless dancer
Now stranded in the stark remains of his
shell.

David

Bronze is the body of gods and heroes:
How the body curves as though a serpent
Entwined on a tree in Eden;
How the hand rests on the hip,
Erotic, relaxed, unphased
By the naked skin beneath;
How the thighs celebrate in sleek seduction
The sensual and the splendid;
How the giant's wing curls about the leg
Teasing the untethered groin;
How the eye is drawn to the center,
The hairless totem soft and smooth
Shamelessly loin caressed.
Bronze is the body of heroes and gods:
Beauty engendered knows no gender.

Kill Devil Hills

The forecast for Kill Devil Hills said beware the breakers
That run like barking dogs on the white foam stretch of beach.
But the tide was too tempting; no mere half measures
Sufficient to restrain the light of romance dancing on crested waves.
So he waded in, salt spray stinging the squinting eyes
Blind to rectitude, blind to his own insouciance.
Waist deep now in water chilling the throbbing blood,
He began with even strokes, until his muscles
Broke like branches, lungs stretched like drum skins.
And the sea coughed him back, waves an endless rocking cradle,
Content in their unconcern, staining the empty strand
With ageless, untamed hand.

Legacy

Strip me of my saddle, nutmeg, and silver
shoe,
Linens to bind my broken heart, monkey
jug,
Money, and a sky of burning blue…
I shall take love where I find it,
Take it, then steal away,
Like Jesus in the brothel
Insisting he will not pay.

Saint Joan

When she said she felt fire, I looked around
for the flame,
But no blaze burned in her empty hearth.
The smoke of her thin nightgown--pastel
leaves and buds--
Lingered in my blood like liqueur, aperitif of
apples and apricots.
And when her aspect became embers,
smoldering in silence,
Beyond the familiar recesses of memory,
I dressed her in ash, gray ghostly cinders
Echoing now in armor abandoned and
hollow.

Softness Comes

Softness comes in hours of uncertain
darkness,
When the dray horse sleeps in his stall,
When the cry of the owl goes unheard,
When the snow sneaks in to cover
Cow and clover in unmown fields.
Softness comes with the mist, silken and
silent
In its morning habitation.
Softness comes in hands, crinkled as granite,
Gray as dreams of death,
Still as exhaled breath.
Softness comes...

Not the Beast but the Cage

Not the beast but the cage becomes the carnivore.
The fly breathes in amber stillness silenced by eons
Of frozen momentum, wings melting to vestigial stumps:
Memory of vague intent, catastrophic longing
Reduced to impotent remnant.
And I...I stand amid stalks of withered corn,
Confined, cribbed--another ear paying yearly tribute
To a clock with iron hands, prison of cosmic bars
Fired with the heat of foreknowing.
The cage is the carnivore,
And I its willing fly.

Part II: An Autobiographical Work in Progress

Innocence

Just as Joyce's North Richmond Street, Harvey Avenue in the 1950's was blind, a narrow nondescript street that ended in the woods and marshes of the Ashley River. It was not an access road to anywhere, just a dead-end road of eleven small houses, shorter in length than a football field. If you stood at the juncture of Azalea Road and Harvey Avenue, you would have seen six houses on the right side, five on the left side. Ours was the first one on the right.

Each house resembled all the others, except in the color of asphalt shingles that covered the exterior. Each one exhibited a small concrete front porch, some screened, but most exposed to the elements. Some windows were shaded by awnings installed by the owners. These were the abodes of working-class people, and the houses reflected that status. The interiors were not elaborate: a small front room leading to three bedrooms, each with hardly enough room for a bed and bureau; a dining room to the right of the living room, and a small kitchen adjacent to the dining area. Only one bathroom serviced for the family, no second bath, half-bath, or any of those amenities people expect now in a home.

But these small houses were *homes*, in the true sense of the word. Inside each one resided a family, a unit. Each one housed a father, a mother, and at least two children…no divorces, no single moms or dads. Most of the fathers worked (as mine did) at the Naval Shipyard. My father had worked there since he left the Navy, a marine machinist working in the bowels of the big ships that came for repair. I can still picture him walking up the road from the bus stop, greasy from his day's labor. But stoic, always stoic in his duty to his family. A proud man, a man with flaws, certainly, but flaws that never eroded his basic humanity or innate integrity. And I suppose the same could be said of all the fathers on that nondescript street of unassuming houses.

And the mothers were always there…soft, stern, healing, nurturing, working from dawn until bedtime without complaint, without expectation of anything more than well-behaved children and a man who came home at the end of the working day. I see mine now as I write this, standing at the counter in that crowded kitchen placing finely crafted dough on the top of a freshly made pie before crimping the edges with artistic precision. Stoic too in her manner, strong Russian-German blood coursing through her veins.

And we, the children, were the beneficiaries of this largesse. Playmates abounded, those of my own age and some older. The older ones, like my brother, no doubt regarded the younger children as unavoidable annoyances to be tolerated and ignored, if possible. But there we all were: Eddie, Bobby, Richie, Freddie, two Jimmys, Beverly, Ginger, Janice, Nancy, Theresa, quite a coterie exploring those narrow precincts of Charleston Heights.

But how those narrow precincts were an empire to us, and we were the kings and queens of those sparse surroundings, each of us a Minos or a Nefertiti in his or her own right. No lease, no deed, no formal contract granted us sovereignty, but in our minds and our actions, we reigned supreme. And there was so much to explore, so much to see, so much to be understood and stored in our youthful memories.

The centerpiece in the backyard of our small lot was a magnificent oak tree, rising and spreading in majesty like some arboreal Henry VIII. During sweet soft summers I would play under its limbs, shaded and sheltered by those stout arms. I was Davy Crockett at the Alamo, Zorro on his black shining steed, the Swamp Fox outwitting the Red Coats, Flash Gordon battling Ming the Merciless. And it was beneath that tree that I would swing on the swing-set my father built, higher and higher as I pumped my small arms on the chains…and sang, sang full-throated and unashamed, as small children do before the world tells them to sit down and shut up.

Music was a visceral thing then. The few stations available on the radio were not confined by genre as stations are now. I could tune into one of our two local stations and hear Hank Williams, Tony Bennet, Jo Stafford, Fats Domino. Even as a small boy, I had memorized many of my favorite tunes. I vividly recall one morning when I was no older than five or six, swinging and singing as I watched a lineman ascend a pole adjacent to our backyard. He shouted requests as he hung from his precarious perch, and I with my tinny voice launched into "Heart of Stone," a tune then riding high on the Hit Parade.

One day around this same time, my father brought home a box packed with 78 RPM recordings someone had given him. I pawed through them like an archaeologist examining the ruins of an ancient civilization. I was captivated by the sunflower yellow MGM labels with the roaring lion at the top. I played and replayed one of them, "Roly Poly," by Hank Williams, until the grooves were worn and the stylus could barely find purchase: "Roly Poly, daddy's little fatty/
Bet he's gonna be a man someday." I suppose in our current politically correct atmosphere, these lyrics would be censored, but back then and back there, they entranced me with their innocence and pure affection.

"Innocence" is the key word here, the word that summons and screens those times, those memories so haunting and so ephemeral. Yes, the world was a threatening place, as it always is. But whatever dangers lurked there, we were shielded from them, such as the scene that unfolded on the black-and-white television screen as I sat watching in total ignorance of its meaning: a map of Europe, over which were superimposed a hammer and sickle spreading their malignant shadow. This emotionally charged scene meant nothing to me then. No, my toys beckoned, and the television image was abandoned.

My favorite toys were playsets by Marx: "Zorro," "Fort Apache," "Battle of the Blue and Gray," "The Alamo," Ben Hur," "Foreign Legion," and the one that paid homage to our forty-ninth state, "Eskimo Village." These sets abounded with realistic figures of people and animals; movable equipment; working weapons in miniature; and finely detailed buildings. I could spend hours enthralled by these, imaging and inventing fantastic scenarios. I could be ice-locked in an igloo with my fellow Eskimos, or I could drive my dog sled to rescue some Eskimo damsel in distress. I could be Ben Hur racing my chariot against the evil machinations of Messala. I was a fearless Foreign Legion soldier fending off invading Arabs, or a dauntless cavalry member standing against marauding Indians.

So many of these sets could not be made now. They appear now and again on ebay or some similar site at exorbitant prices as collectors' items. I never saw them, of course, as an investment. To me they were doorways into fantasy and imagination. And I do believe they helped stamp and form elements of my personality, particularly, a penchant for solitary pursuits and a tendency to imagine fantastic events in rich detail.

In addition to the toys, there were books and comics to capture the imagination of a small boy. Big Little Books were among my favorites, small books perfect for small hands, but pathways to a broader world. And with them, the discovery in my elementary school library of a series focused on the lives of great Americans. These were thin, unassuming tomes, all bound in blue cloth with gold lettering. But such riches inside: Washington, Jefferson, Francis Marion, Lincoln…all took on human form and became real in my imagination. That small library in a small school was a haven. I checked out books on knights, the French Foreign Legion, dinosaurs, the Arctic…anything that captured my curiosity.

And then there came Classics Illustrated comic books. These were my introduction to great literature in abbreviated form, complete with richly colored illustrations. I sailed with Odysseus, battled at Troy, followed Quasimodo through the streets of Paris, earned my own Red Badge of Courage, trudged in the mud on the Western Front, hurled harpoons as I listened to the ravings of Ahab. These slim comics paved the way to great books later in my life.

All of these were outlets for the imagination to bloom. And in addition to these, there were radio dramas before we purchased our first television. I listened to *Gunsmoke* and pictured the gunfights in my mind. *Inner Sanctum* held me spellbound and frightened as I heard that creaking door that started each episode. What was entering in such stealth? What human or inhuman creature was creeping from the shadows? Only in my imagination did these phantoms take form. I created and colored them as only a five or six-year old can.

I am speaking now of memory, imperfect yet precise. I excavate memory layer by layer, peeling back each stratum to reveal experiences covered by the detritus of time, forsaken but not forgotten. I am not to be held responsible for slippage, nor for embellishments that have wedged their way into these memories, now more than six decades old. But is their value decreased by these odd additions, or are they more precious coinage because of the random addition? You cannot know, nor can I; memories are now set, the canon is solidified. So I lay these experiences before you to accept or reject.

Experience

But all was not light and innocence in our protected little domain. No, the world will always find a way to intrude, an avenue of darkness to insinuate itself. I was too young to appreciate fully these intrusions, but they were there, and they were manifest.

One summer day just at twilight, after a busy day of playing my youthful games, I stood on our side porch as my mother busied herself in the kitchen preparing evening supper. Suddenly, a line of cars appeared on Azalea Road, moving slowly like a snake through tall grass. Each car had its dome light illuminated, so each interior was visible. Four riders sat in each car, two in the front seat and two in back. Each face was obscured by a tall white hood which contained eye holes only. I could tell each rider was wearing a white robe. My childish imagination saw them as ghosts, spirits perhaps from the cemetery that abutted our backyard.

In total innocence I said to my mother through the screen door, “I see ghosts in cars." She looked out the door; her aspect changed immediately. "They are not ghosts," she replied. "Come in now and close the door." I knew from her tone I needed to comply. "But who are they?" I asked. Her response was curt but spoke volumes: "Bad men." She need say no more. Even though I did not know who they were or why they were dressed so strangely, I understood her words in a visceral way. And those two words have echoed in my mind these decades later.

I have alluded to our yard being adjacent to a cemetery, Riverview Memorial, to be exact. I could walk directly from our backyard into the graveyard, no fence or partition to impede my way. It was a big, rambling place with serpentine pathways winding through it. One side was bordered by the Ashley River. For me, the cemetery was a perfect place for solitary wandering, for thinking, for allowing my imagination to stroll wherever it wanted.

Within its loose boundaries, the cemetery was a visual reminder of life's frailty and brevity. In the central portion was a section containing graves from the nineteenth century, markers weather-worn and almost illegible. Another section was reserved for infants and toddlers. For me, this section was the saddest. Some plots held babies who had lived for mere minutes, hours, or days. Some had lived for a few short years before accident, disease, or violence took them. But they were all robbed, robbed of a life that was their due.

And here was I, solitary witness to the mortality none of us shall escape. Whether for centenarian or for toddler, death comes too soon, a stalking presence waiting, waiting. Whether freshly turned or ancient, the dirt on the grave is the same. And flowers cannot disguise the stench of decay. Here were the dark lessons I embraced early.

The far side of the cemetery was a stand of trees, mostly pine and oak, forming a barrier to vision. I never saw with witness of my eyes what lay beyond those trees. But I came to learn what was there through other means. And the sad reality was palpable.

I see it clearly in my memory: a mother walking by the road that led to the gates of the cemetery. But that was not her destination. Beyond those gates, beyond the stand of oak and pine lay the entrance to an edifice: Jenkins Orphanage. By her side walked a child, perhaps four or five years old. The faces of both mother and child exhibiting pain, sadness, and the grim acceptance of a reality too real to acknowledge except in thin trails of tears on their stoic black faces.

So many times in the heat of a summer afternoon, one such couple would pause in their dismal sojourn, worn down from both the blistering heat and the unspeakable burden of life. My mother, always compassionate and caring, would offer them a cold glass of water to slake their thirst. But some thirsts run too deep to be slaked by mere water.

I knew that in a few brief minutes, they would enter the orphanage. The child would be left there with a few meager belongings. The mother would retrace her steps, this time in reverse, a steady stream of tears flowing now, unstoppable in the face of an inevitable truth.

I would think often of that child and the others left at the orphanage. I could sense their crying in the darkness, crying for love lost, crying for the ugliness of life, crying perhaps for a situation they did not fully comprehend at their tender age. But I know I felt a sadness, a sadness I too did not fully comprehend. As I grew older and learned to observe, the sadness would remain, and added to it would be anger, anger at a world that would force a mother to abandon her child to the unknown…trapped, confined, caged by a system of indifference and cruelty.

So yes, elements of darkness were present in my childhood world of games, songs, and youthful pursuits. But I suppose, like all children, I wanted nothing more than the freedom to be a child, running, climbing, pedaling my bike with nothing more than a skinned knee to break the brightness of my days.

But always that other child was there in my mind, sometimes sleeping, sometimes wide awake. And no matter how high my swing would lift me, I would never escape the bonds of the world that grew tighter and more confining as I aged.

www.ingramcontent.com/pod-product-compliance
Lightning Source LLC
LaVergne TN
LVHW040952150826
845672LV00002B/662

9798351732404